FRANCE

Anita Ganeri
and Rachel Wright

SEA-TO-SEA

Mankato Collingwood London

This edition first published in 2006 by
Sea-to-Sea Publications
1980 Lookout Drive
North Mankato
Minnesota 56003

Printed in China

Library of Congress Cataloging-in-Publication Data

Ganeri, Anita, 1961-
   France / by Anita Ganeri & Rachel Wright.
      p. cm. — (Country topics)
   Includes index.
   ISBN 1-932889-91-4
      1. France—Civilization—20th century—Juvenile literature. I. Wright, Rachel. II. Title.
III. Country topics (Sea to Sea Publications)

DC33.7.G338 2005
944—dc22

2004063713

9 8 7 6 5 4 3 2

Published by arrangement with the Watts Publishing Group Ltd, London

Editor: Hazel Poole
Designer: Sally Boothroyd
Photography: Peter Millard
Artwork: John Shackell and Teri Gower
Picture research: Ambreen Husain, Annabel Martin, Juliet Duff

CONTENTS

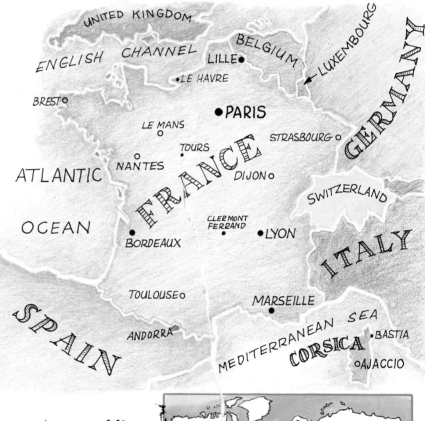

BIENVENUE A LA FRANCE!

Welcome to France! Before you start to explore, here are a few useful facts about the country.

FRANCE IN THE WORLD

France is the second-biggest country in Western Europe, covering an area of about 224,037 square miles (544,000 sq km), including the island of Corsica. Its capital is Paris, one of the world's most famous and glamorous cities. As you can see from the map, France has a long coastline with the Atlantic Ocean and Mediterranean Sea. On land, it has borders with Spain, Italy, Switzerland, Germany, Luxembourg, and Belgium. It is separated from Great Britain by the English Channel.

FLYING THE FLAG

The French flag is called *le tricolore* (the tricolor) because it has three stripes of blue, red, and white. The colors have special meanings. Red and blue are the colors of Paris and white was once the color of French royalty. The present flag was first used in the French Revolution of 1789.

France is a republic – its official title is *République Française*. The president is the head of state and is elected for seven years at a time. The prime minister leads the government. Parliament is made up of the National Assembly and the Senate.

FRENCH MONEY AND STAMPS

The French currency is called the *euro*, written as €. One euro is divided into 100 cents (c). You can get euro bills for the following amounts: 5, 10, 20, 50, 100, 200, and 500 euros. There are coins for 1 and 2 euros, as well as for 1, 2, 5, 10, 20, and 50 euro cents.

French stamps haven't escaped from the influence of the French Revolution. They show the figure of a woman, known as Marianne, an emblem of the Revolution.

> On one side of French coins are the words, *Liberté, Egalité, Fraternité*–Liberty, Equality, Fraternity–the motto of the French Revolution.

LA MARSEILLAISE

The French national anthem is called *La Marseillaise*. It was composed by a solider, Claude-Joseph Rouget De Lisle, as a rousing marching song for the revolutionary army as they walked from Marseille to Paris in 1792. It became the national song in 1795, and the national anthem in 1879.

KEEP TO THE RIGHT

In France, you drive on the right-hand side of the street so cars have their steering wheels on the left. You can tell which part of France a car comes from by its license plate. Different *départements* (regions) have their own numbers, which they use on cars and as postal codes.

> **Say it in French**
> *le drapeau* - flag
> *le timbre* - stamp
> *l'argent* - money
> *la France* - France
> *les Français* - the French
> *la carte* - map

5

Around France

There are many different parts of France to visit–rolling countryside, snow-capped mountains, tree-lined rivers, and sandy beaches. There are also many ancient buildings and historic landmarks to see.

Average temperatures		
Place	January	July
Paris	32° F	75° F
Nice	48° F	80° F
Bordeaux	45° F	78° F

WHAT DIALECT?

Several different languages and dialects are spoken in France. It all depends on the area. For example, in parts of Brittany, some people speak a language known as Breton, and in the area around the border with Spain you can hear Basque being spoken. Also, in the Alsace and Lorraine regions, a German dialect can be heard.

MONT-ST-MICHEL

Mont-St-Michel is a small island off the coast of Normandy. At high tide, the island is surrounded by water. At low tide, however, you can drive or walk to it across the seabed. Millions of people a year visit the picturesque abbey and town on the island.

FRENCH GEOGRAPHY

The landscape of France changes from place to place. This map shows the main geographical regions and the main mountains and rivers. It also shows a few famous places you might like to visit.

Like the scenery, the weather also varies from place to place. The north of France has warm summers and cold winters. The south has very hot summers and mild winters. It is also wetter in the north. Mountainous areas in the east and south have heavy snow in winter.

July and August are the hottest months of the year. The south is sometimes hit by a fierce, cold wind called the *mistral* which can destroy farmers' crops.

EIFFEL TOWER

The Eiffel Tower is one of Paris's most famous landmarks. It was built for the Paris *Exposition* (exhibition) of 1889 and contains 9,700 tons of iron. It is 1,000 feet (300.5 m) high. It's a steep climb to the top but you get a good view of the city.

THE FRENCH RIVIERA

The sunny south coast is famous for its resorts, such as Nice and Cannes. These attract tourists from all over the world–often very wealthy ones! This stretch of coastline is known as the Riviera or the Côte d'Azur–the sky-blue coast.

MONT BLANC

Mont Blanc is the highest mountain in the Alps, at 15,781 feet (4,810 m). The nearby town of Chamonix is popular with mountaineers and skiers. The first winter Olympics were held in Chamonix in 1924. Other famous ski resorts include Val d'Isère and Courchevel.

CHATEAU DE CHAMBORD

The River Loire is famous for its beautiful stately homes, or châteaux. The château of Chambord was built by King François I in 1519. It is a mass of turrets, chimneys, and bell towers. It has more than 15 staircases. One is a double spiral–two people can walk up or down it without ever meeting!

Say it in French

l'été - summer	la pluie - rain
l'hiver - winter	la plage - beach
le temps - weather	la montagne - mountain
le soleil - sun	la tour Eiffel - Eiffel tower
le château - castle, stately home	

Food and Drink

rench restaurants, food, and drink are famous all over the world. In France itself, food is taken very seriously indeed.

SHOPPING FOR FOOD

rench people love food and take a lot of trouble over what they eat. They are careful about what they buy, spending time and money on finding the freshest, tastiest ingredients. Most people go to the supermarket once a week, but they also visit small, specialty shops and the local market. Every French town has its market day, when farmers sell their fresh fruit, vegetables, eggs and cheese. There are street markets in big cities, such as Paris, too.

Shopping list
le pain - bread
le lait - milk
le fromage - cheese
les oeufs - eggs
le sucre - sugar
les légumes - vegetables
le poisson - fish
le café - coffee
le vin - wine
le chocolat - chocolate

rance is also famous for its wine, champagne, and brandy. There are several important wine-growing areas, such as the Loire valley, where you can see vineyards for miles around.

Boulangeries sell all kinds of bread. The long French stick, called a *baguette*, is crisp outside and chewy inside.

Patisseries sell wonderful cakes and pastries. Try a fruit *tarte* or a cream-filled *éclair*.

Charcuteries sell cooked meats, sausages, and *pâté*.

Fromageries are special shops selling cheese. There are over 300 kinds of French cheese, made from cow's, sheep's, and goat's milk.

FRENCH COOKING

French chefs are famous for their cooking skills. The food varies a little in each part of France because chefs make use of the different local ingredients. In the north, where cows graze on the lush grass, lots of butter and cream are used. Brittany is famous for its *crêpes*. Along the coasts seafood is very popular, with dishes such as *bouillabaisse* (fish soup) and *moules* (mussels). Further south, food is flavored with local herbs, garlic, and olive oil.

As well as cooking at home, French people enjoy eating out in cafés and restaurants. The whole family may go to a restaurant for lunch at the weekend. The meal will consist of three or four courses–for example soup, meat or fish with vegetables, cheese, and fruit or a dessert to finish.

People take their time over their food–lunch may last the whole afternoon!

CROISSANT MAZE

You have been kidnapped by food fanatics and locked up in the sugar room of a croissant factory. To make your escape, you can only enter those rooms which are named after a food or drink. You have 60 seconds to make your getaway... starting now!

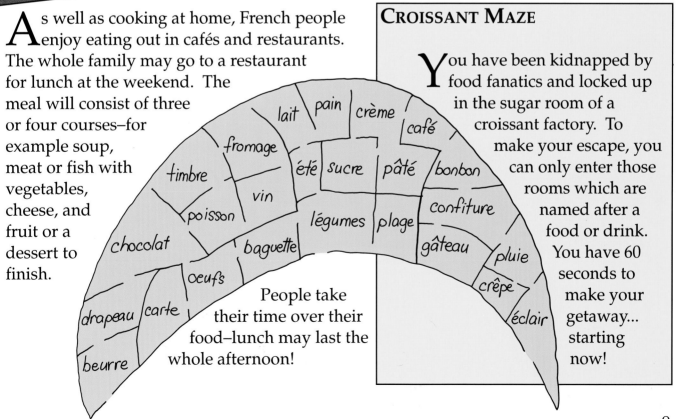

Maze labels: lait, pain, crème, café, fromage, été, sucre, pâté, bonbon, timbre, vin, confiture, poisson, légumes, plage, chocolat, baguette, gâteau, pluie, oeufs, crêpe, drapeau, carte, éclair, beurre

9

A Taste of France

French cafés are famous for their terraces, where customers can relax with a drink or a snack and watch the world go by. Most cafés display a list of snacks in their window. These usually include pizza, omelettes, baguette sandwiches, and *croque-monsieur*.

Croque-monsieur is easy to make and delicious to eat, as you'll discover if you try the recipe below.

YOU WILL NEED:

TWO THICK SLICES OF BREAD

TWO THIN SLICES OF HARD CHEESE
(ABOUT THE SAME SIZE AS THE BREAD)

A FAIRLY LARGE SLICE OF HAM

KNIFE

BUTTER

FRYING PAN

METAL SPATULA

PAPER TOWELS

1. Butter both slices of bread on both sides.

2. Cover one of the pieces of bread with a slice of cheese. Then add the ham, the other slice of cheese, and the second slice of bread –to make a double-decker sandwich.

3. Melt a small lump of butter in the frying pan over a low heat.

4. Fry the sandwich for three to five minutes on each side until the bread is golden brown and the cheese is beginning to melt.

5. When your sandwich is ready, carefully lift it out of the pan with the metal spatula, drain it on some paper towels and dig in!

Croque monsieur means "Mr. Crunch!"

10

Cafés in France sell a wide range of hot and cold drinks, including *citron pressé*, or freshly squeezed lemonade.

To make your own *citron pressé*...

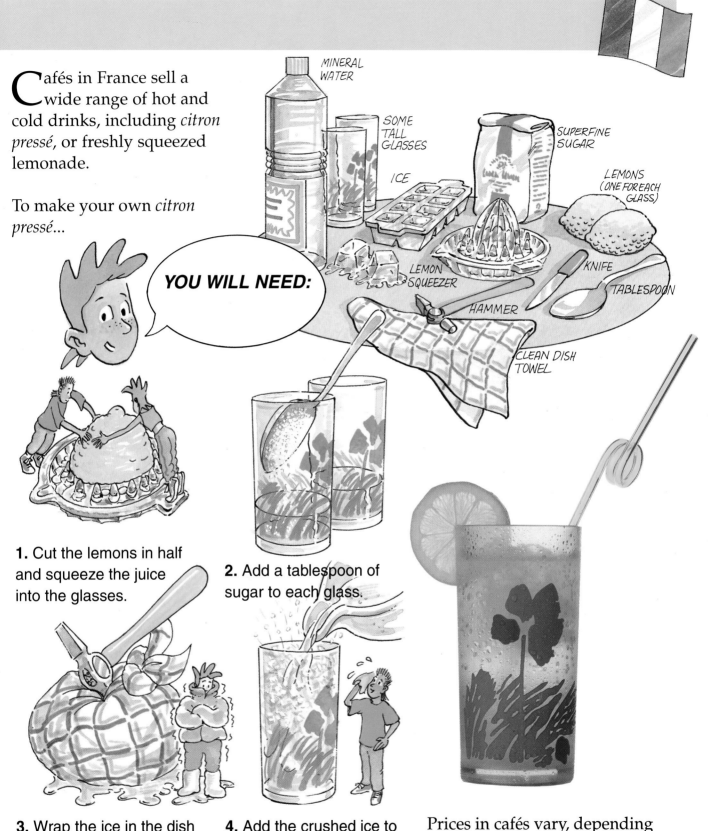

YOU WILL NEED:

MINERAL WATER
SOME TALL GLASSES
ICE
SUPERFINE SUGAR
LEMONS (ONE FOR EACH GLASS)
LEMON SQUEEZER
KNIFE
TABLESPOON
HAMMER
CLEAN DISH TOWEL

1. Cut the lemons in half and squeeze the juice into the glasses.

2. Add a tablespoon of sugar to each glass.

3. Wrap the ice in the dish towel and tap it carefully with the hammer until it is crushed.

4. Add the crushed ice to the sugar and juice. Fill each glass with water and serve at once.

Prices in cafés vary, depending on whether you sit at a table inside, stand at the bar, or sit outside on the terrace.

Life in France

WHERE PEOPLE LIVE

Almost three quarters of French people live in towns and cities. Many live in apartments–either in old buildings in the center of town or in modern housing complexes on the outskirts. In many French cities there are laws forbidding the building of high-rise buildings in the city center. People often live in the suburbs and commute into the city every day to work.

About one quarter of French people live in the countryside, many in small villages. These usually have a village square, with a church and some small stores. Houses are often small and traditional with shutters at the windows. Some people live in farmhouses.

WHAT PEOPLE DO

Many people in the big cities work in factories making cars, electronic goods, and aircraft. In the countryside, some people are farmers. They raise sheep and cows, and grow crops such as wheat, apples, grapes, and sugar beet. In Paris, the Alps and along the Côte d'Azur, many people are employed in the tourist industry.

POLICE

In France, there are two kinds of police. *Les gendarmes* work in the country, and *les agents de police* work in the town. The emergency telephone number for the police is 17.

SAY IT IN FRENCH
le fermier - farmer
le professeur - teacher
le médecin - doctor
l'ouvrier - factory worker
le chef - chef
le facteur - mailman

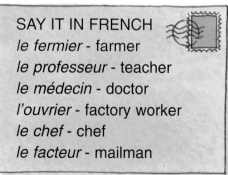

GOING TO SCHOOL

French children must go to school from the ages of 6 - 16. From 6 - 11 years old they attend primary school; from 11-15, they go to a college. Many then go to a secondary school, or *lycée* to study for the *baccalauréat* or to train for a job. The *"bac"* is a very tough exam–you have to pass it to go on to university. The school day often starts at 8:30 am and finishes at 5:30 pm. There is a two-hour break for lunch. Lessons last for 55 minutes each, with five minutes in between to get from one classroom to the next. Children often go to school on Saturday mornings too, although they have a day off on Wednesday.

anglais	8.30 - 9.25
français	9.30 - 10.25
sciences	10.30 - 11.25
mathématiques	11.30 - 12.25
Le déjeuner	12.30 - 2.30
histoire	2.30 - 3.25
géographie	3.30 - 4.25

USEFUL SHOPS

France is famous for its hypermarkets–huge supermarkets where you can buy anything and everything. In contrast, there are the *Bar-Tabacs*. These are small bars that sell beer and wine, coffee, snacks, postage stamps, and bus or train tickets.

KEEPING INFORMED

French people like to know what is happening in the world and enjoy discussing events. There are 85 daily newspapers to choose from, including *Le Monde, Le Figaro,* and *France-Soir.* There are also magazines, such as *Paris-Match* and *L'Express.* The most popular magazine is *Télé 7 Jours,* a guide that tells people what's on television!

Say it in French
l'école - school
l'église - church
les devoirs - homework
le journal - newspaper
le travail - work
l'usine - factory
la maison - house

13

French Style

FRENCH FASHION

Paris is one of the fashion centers of the world. Each spring, French designers show their latest collections in Paris. They range from the classic style of Yves Saint Laurent to the more unusual designs of Jean-Paul Gaultier. Designers, models, fashion buyers, and fashion writers come from far and wide to see the shows. The Paris collection influences fashion all over the world and sets the trend for the year to come.

French *haute couture* (fashion) and perfumes are world-famous. Even the word *chic* is French!

Lavender grows in plenty in the fields of Provence.

The designs of Jean-Paul Gaultier are guaranteed to make an impression.

Classical elegance is the style set by Yves St. Laurent.

FRENCH PERFUMES

The major fashion houses also create and sell their own brands of perfumes. They include Dior, Chanel, and Givenchy. France has had a perfume industry since the sixteenth century. Grasse in southern France is the center of the industry. To create its perfumes, it uses locally grown wild lavender, jasmine, and violets and imported flowers such as roses, mimosa, and orange blossom.

Say it in French
les vêtements - clothes
la robe - dress
le chapeau - hat
les souliers - shoes
la fleur - flower
le parfum - perfume

Perfumed Jewelry

Try creating your own designer jewelry using perfumed petal beads.

YOU WILL NEED:

4 HANDFULS OF DRIED CHAMOMILE FLOWERS

2 HANDFULS OF FRESH OR DRIED ROSE PETALS

SMALL SAUCEPAN

NEEDLE THREADED WITH THIN BEAD THREAD

NECKLACE FASTENER

BLENDER OR FOOD PROCESSOR

1. Put the chamomile flowers and rose petals into the saucepan and add just enough water to cover them.

2. Ask an adult to heat the water to just below boiling point and let your ingredients simmer for an hour. Check the saucepan regularly to make sure that the water isn't boiling. If the water level drops, add more to just cover the petals.

3. After an hour, turn off the heat and pour your ingredients into the blender. Mix for a minute and then scoop the mixture out of the blender with a spatula.

4. Squeeze the mixture in your hands as hard as you can to get rid of any excess water.

5. Roll the mixture into beads and leave them somewhere warm to dry. This will take about three days.

6. When your beads are bone-dry, string them together. Push the needle through each bead very carefully, otherwise they will crack. (If you're feeling very artistic you could try adding other types of beads into your necklace as well.)

7. To finish, attach the ends of the bead thread to the fastener. If you knot the thread ends and fastener together, put a spot of glue on each knot to fix it in place.

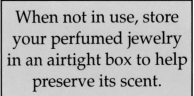

When not in use, store your perfumed jewelry in an airtight box to help preserve its scent.

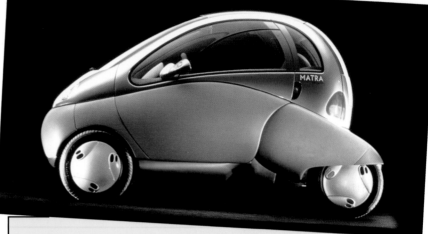

France is a world leader in science and technology. It has a thriving car and aircraft industry and also uses its technological know-how in many other ways.

FRANCE ON THE MOVE

Renault's latest creation, designed to be energy-saving, is the electric car. For easy parking, the rear wheels fold in.

France is the fourth biggest car producer in the world, next to the United States, Japan, and Germany. Among its best-known cars are Renault, Peugeot, and Citroën. They are exported to many other countries. French car designers are always looking for new ideas and styles. One of the very latest Renault designs is an environmentally friendly electric car.

The French railroad system, SNCF (*Société Nationale des Chemins de Fer*) prides itself on its fast, modern trains. The TGV (*Train à Grande Vitesse*) is the world's fastest passenger train, with an average speed of over 137 mph (220 km/h). The first TGV came into service in 1983. They now run between all the major cities in France.

FRANCE IN SPACE

France is a key member of the European Space Agency (ESA) that was founded in 1975. ESA's latest venture was to send the Huygens space probe to Titan, one of the moons of Saturn. After traveling for seven years, it finally landed in January of 2005.

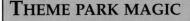

THE CHANNEL TUNNEL

The idea of an undersea tunnel linking Great Britain and France was first suggested in 1802. Work finally started on the Channel Tunnel in 1987 and it began full operations in 1994. Specially designed trains carry people, cars, and freight under the seabed from Folkestone in England to Calais in France. The journey from London to Paris takes just $3^{1}/_{4}$ hours.

THEME PARK MAGIC

French technology has also been put into action at two theme parks– EuroDisney, near Paris, and Futuroscope, near Poitiers. EuroDisney was opened in 1992. Thanks to lasers, video, computers, and other technological magic, visitors can explore four fantasy worlds and meet famous Disney characters such as Mickey and Goofy.

Futuroscope is another theme park that combines the latest technology with having fun. Here you can travel through space, explore the future, and sit in a theater where the seats move or where you are entirely surrounded by the screen.

Say it in French

la voiture - car
le train - train
l'avion - aircraft
l'espace - space
le voyage - journey
le métro - subway

The Sporty French

French people enjoy sports and follow it closely. Some very famous sporting events take place each year in France.

LE MANS

Sports cars competing in the Le Mans 24-hour race drive all night and all day at speeds of over 250 mph (400 km/h).

SOCCER AND RUGBY

Soccer is the most popular team sport in France. The fortunes of the national team and of league teams, such as Marseille, are often the subject of heated discussions! The French rugby union team is one of the best in the world. Each year it competes in the Six Nations' Championship against England, Scotland, Wales, Italy, and Ireland.

TENNIS TOURNAMENT

The Roland Garros Stadium in Paris is the scene of the French Open tennis championship in May. This is one of the four Grand Slam tennis events alongside Wimbledon, the U.S. Open, and the Australian Open.

TOUR DE FRANCE

Each summer, more than 100 professional cyclists take part in the Tour de France bicycle race. It follows a 2,975-mile (4,800-km) course. The route changes each year. The riders race each day for three weeks, and spectators line the route.

HORSE RACING

The *Prix de l'Arc de Triomphe* is one of the most famous and prestigious horse races in the world. It is run at the Longchamp racecourse in Paris.

Say it in French
le tennis - tennis
le football - soccer
le cheval - horse
l'équipe - team
le jeu - game
la course - race
la bicyclette - bicycle
le vélo - bicycle

Boules for Beginners

If you stroll through a village or town square in France on a summer's evening you will probably see a group of people playing *boules*. *Boules*, or *pétanque*, is the national game of France. It is played with metal balls and a jack ball. The object of the game is to toss or roll the *boules* as close to the jack as possible.

boule　○ *jack ball*

Boules is played between two teams of either one, two, or three players. Single players have three or four *boules* each. Players in teams of two have three *boules* each, and players in teams of three have two each.

1. To start, a player from team A draws a circle to stand in and throws the jack 18 - 30 feet (5.5 - 10 m) in front of them. Then they throw their first *boule* as close to the jack as possible. Their feet must stay inside the circle.

2. A player from team B then steps into the circle and tries to throw their *boule* closer to the jack or to knock the other *boule* away.

3. It is up to whichever team is not winning at this stage to keep throwing their *boules* until one lands nearest to the jack. Then it is the other team's turn. When a team has no *boules* left to play, the other team throws its remaining *boules*.

4. When neither team has any *boules* left, the score is added up. The team with the *boule* closest to the jack scores one point for each *boule* which is better placed than the opposing team's best *boule*. For example, if team A has two *boules* nearer to the jack than team B's best placed *boule*, team A scores two points.

5. At the end of each round, the winning team draws another circle, throws the jack, and starts a new round. The first team to reach 13 points is the winner.

Holidays and Festivals

The French have a wide variety of holidays and festivals including national holidays such as Christmas, saints' days, and local fairs and festivals.

HAPPY CHRISTMAS!

Christmas is celebrated in various ways in different parts of France. In Alsace and Lorraine, people put up and decorate Christmas trees. In Provence, they have a crib *(crèche)* with wooden nativity figures *(santons)*. People do not usually give their presents on Christmas Day. They give them on St. Nicholas's Day (December 6) or on *la Fête des Rois* (January 6). A special cake is eaten on *la Fête des Rois*. It contains a bean or a tiny plastic figure. If you get the bean or figure in your piece of cake, you are king or queen for the day.

BASTILLE DAY

July 14 is a national holiday in France. It is the anniversary of the storming of the Bastille prison in Paris in 1789. This marked the start of the French Revolution. On Bastille Day there is a grand military procession in Paris, fireworks, and dancing.

FETES AND FESTIVALS

There are hundreds of local festivals all over France. Some celebrate saints' days. Others celebrate farming events such as the grape or lavender harvest, or local produce such as snails, cheese, and oysters. In Brittany, people celebrate festivals called *Pardons* to honor their local saints. They dress in traditional costume (right) and perform traditional folk dances.

EN VACANCES

French people are entitled to five weeks' vacation a year. They usually take time off in July and August. Then the roads are packed with people heading for the coast, the mountains, or the countryside.

FILM FESTIVAL

Each year in May, an international film festival is held in Cannes in the south of France. Famous film stars, directors, and producers come to see the latest films debut. Prizes are awarded to the best films and the best actors.

MARDI GRAS

The town of Nice holds a huge carnival each year to mark the two weeks before Lent begins. The streets are filled with brightly decorated floats and people in fancy costumes. There are brass bands, fireworks, and flower battles.

Say it in French
les vacances - vacation
la fête - festival
le Noël - Christmas
les Pâques - Easter
l'anniversaire - birthday

Make a Carnival Mask

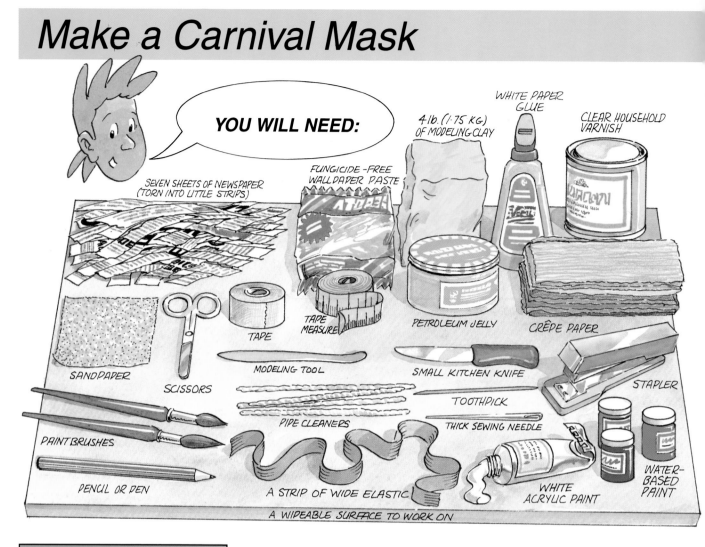

YOU WILL NEED:

SEVEN SHEETS OF NEWSPAPER
(TORN INTO LITTLE STRIPS)

FUNGICIDE-FREE
WALLPAPER PASTE

4 lb. (1.75 KG)
OF MODELING CLAY

WHITE PAPER
GLUE

CLEAR HOUSEHOLD
VARNISH

TAPE

TAPE
MEASURE

PETROLEUM JELLY

CRÊPE PAPER

SANDPAPER

SCISSORS

MODELING TOOL

SMALL KITCHEN KNIFE

STAPLER

PAINT BRUSHES

PIPE CLEANERS

TOOTHPICK

THICK SEWING NEEDLE

PENCIL OR PEN

A STRIP OF WIDE ELASTIC

WHITE
ACRYLIC PAINT

WATER-
BASED
PAINT

A WIPEABLE SURFACE TO WORK ON

To make the modeling clay mold

1. Hold the tape measure under your chin and measure all the way around your face. Make a note of this measurement.

2. Knead the modeling clay to make it warm. Then roll some of it into sausages and use these to make the outline of a face. The circumference of this shape should be about the same as your face measurement.

3. Fill in the outline with small lumps of clay until it looks like a flat-topped mound.

22

4. Hold the clay mold against your face and carefully mark the position of your eyes and mouth. Using these markings as a guide, cut holes for your eyes and mouth with the knife. Shape and smooth the edges of these holes with the modeling tool.

5. Model a nose, chin, and cheeks from small lumps of clay and join them to the mold with the modeling tool. Use the modeling tool to carve eye sockets as well.

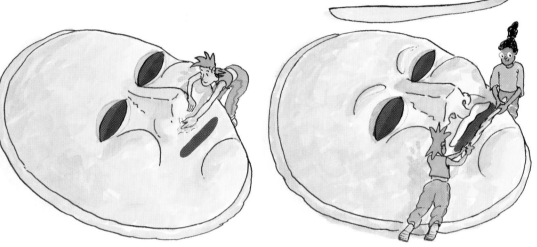

6. To make lips and eyelids, shape small lumps of clay into rolls and join them to the mold with the modeling tool.

To make the pâpier maché mask

7. Cover the surface of your mold with a layer of petroleum jelly. Now add a layer of newspaper strips dipped in the wallpaper paste. Wait for the glued paper to dry and add another layer. Your mask will need about seven layers in total. (Make sure that each layer is dried out completely before you apply the next one.)

8. When the final layer of paper is dry, ease the mask away from its mold. Gently rub it with sandpaper to make it smooth, and paint it with white acrylic paint. This acrylic undercoat will help your topcoat of paint stay bright.

9. Once the undercoat has dried, you can paint your mask any color you like. If you want your mask to have a shiny finish, cover it with a coat of clear gloss varnish once the paint has dried.

There are lots of ways to decorate your mask, but if you want to wear it for *un carnaval de Pâques* why not liven it up with some paper spring flowers?

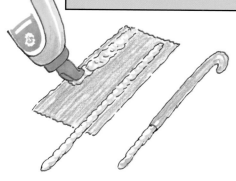  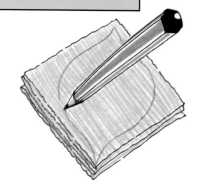

10. Glue a length of green crêpe paper around two-thirds of a pipe cleaner to make a stem. Bend the top of the pipe cleaner over into a small hook.

11. Cut a strip of crêpe paper into a fringe and wind it around the hooked end of the pipe cleaner. Secure the fringe to the stem with tape.

12. Fold some crêpe paper in half several times. Draw a petal shape and cut it out. You will have lots of identical petals which you can then tape onto your flower stem, one at a time.

13. When you've added as many petals as you need, glue a small rectangle of green crêpe paper around their base to cover the tape.

To attach each flower

14. Pierce the rim of your mask with the needle and widen the hole with the toothpick. Push your flower stem into the hole and tape it to the back of your mask. Make and secure more flowers in the same way.

15. When your mask is complete, staple the strip of elastic to its sides, making sure that the jagged ends of each staple are on the outside. Now put on your mask and get set to celebrate.

If you want to add a frill or veil, cut a piece of lace or netting to the right length and attach it to the edges of your mask.

The Arts

French culture has produced many masterpieces of writing and art. Here you can find out about just a few of them.

Victor Hugo (1802 - 1850)

Paul Gauguin (1848 - 1903)

Victor Hugo wrote poems, novels, and plays. His two most famous novels are *The Hunchback of Notre Dame* and *Les Misérables*. When he died in 1885, all of France went into mourning.

When Gauguin was 35 years old, he left his job as a stockbroker to become a painter. He later traveled to Tahiti where his work was inspired by the people and bright colors of the South Sea islands.

Molière wrote comedies based on people's weaknesses and odd behavior. For example, *Le Malade Imaginaire* is about a hypochondriac, and *Le Misanthrope* is about a man who didn't get along with anyone except himself.

One of Rodin's most famous sculptures is *The Thinker*. It is now on display in the Rodin Museum in Paris.

Auguste Rodin (1840 - 1917)

Molière (1622 - 1673)

Say it in French
le livre - book
l'artiste - artist
la peinture - painting
l'écrivain - writer
le stylo - pen
le papier - paper

Dabs and Dashes

This painting, called *Impression, Sunrise,* was painted by Claude Monet. When it was first exhibited in Paris in 1874, alongside other paintings in a similar style, art critics threw up their hands in horror. This new style of painting was far too vague for their liking and so they nicknamed the artists "Impressionists."

Although invented as an insult to Monet and his colleagues, the term "Impressionism" suited their style of painting well. Unlike most artists at that time, the Impressionists were more interested in capturing the atmosphere of a scene than portraying a lifelike image of it. In particular, they wanted to show how sunlight affects the color and shape of an object. To achieve this, they painted in dabs and dashes, avoiding neat outlines, and mixed the colors on their canvases rather than on their palettes.

One of the quickest ways to capture an impression of a scene is to paint it onto dampened white paper. Choose an outdoor scene that looks interesting in the sunlight and find a comfortable spot from which to paint it. When you've decided which colors you are going to use, brush some clean water over your paper and apply your paint quickly in dabs. The wetter your paper, the farther your paint will flow. If part of your paper dries out before you can paint on it, just wet it again. Be careful, as wet paper is very fragile and will tear easily.

If you can, go back to your chosen scene at a different time of the day and paint it again. The change in sunlight should give you a whole new set of colors and shadows to paint.

French History

France is an old country with a long and sometimes turbulent history. Here are some of the key events and characters.

THE ROMANS

Julius Caesar and his Roman army conquered France in 58 B.C. The country was known as Gaul. There are many Roman remains in France, including amphitheaters and aqueducts. The Roman conquest also inspired the later adventures of the cartoon character *Astérix*. His village holds out against the Romans, thanks to a magic potion that gives the villagers superhuman strength!

THE NORMAN CONQUEST

In A.D. 895, Normandy in northern France was invaded by Vikings from Norway and Denmark. They became known as the Normans. The Norman king, William (the Conqueror), defeated the English king, Harold, at the Battle of Hastings in 1066 and became king of England.

JOAN OF ARC

When she was a young girl, Joan of Arc (Jeanne d'Arc) heard the voice of God telling her to save France and restore the French king to his rightful throne. At that time, France was under English rule. Joan obeyed and in 1429 led the French army to victory at the town of Orléans. The following year, however, she was taken prisoner by the English and later burned at the stake. The Roman Catholic church made her into a saint in 1920.

Vive la Révolution!

On July 14, 1789, the Bastille prison in Paris was stormed by ordinary French people. They were tired of being hungry and poor while the French king lived in luxury. The French Revolution had begun. The king, Louis XVI, his queen, Marie Antoinette, and many other royal and noble people were sent to the guillotine. France became a republic.

Napoleon Bonaparte

Napoléon Bonaparte (1769-1821) was a brilliant army general who had himself crowned emperor of France in 1804. He was eventually defeated by the Duke of Wellington at the Battle of Waterloo in 1815. He was sent into exile on the island of St. Helena in the South Atlantic. He died there in 1821. His remains now lie in the *Hôtel des Invalides* in Paris.

General de Gaulle

During World War II, Charles de Gaulle (1890-1970) was the leader of the Free French, or French Resistance, against the Nazis. In 1958, he became the first president of the Fifth Republic in France. He negotiated the independence of Algeria from France in 1962 and had a great influence on French politics. He resigned in 1969.

Say it in French
l'histoire - history
le roi - king
le soldat - soldier
la bataille - battle
le président - president
la politique - politics

TIME BAND

58 B.C. Romans invade France
A.D.486 Roman Empire collapses; Franks conquer
A.D.768 - 814 Reign of Charlemagne
A.D.895 Vikings settle in Normandy
1337 - 1453 Hundred Years War between France and England
1431 Jeanne d'Arc is burned at the stake in Rouen
1643 - 1715 Reign of Louis XIV, the Sun King

1789 - 1792 French Revolution
1792 The First Republic
1799 Napoléon comes to power
1815 Napoléon is defeated at the Battle of Waterloo
1848 - 1852 The Second Republic
1871 - 1946 The Third Republic
1914 - 1918 World War I
1939 - 1945 World War II
1940 - 1944 Germany occupies France
1946 - 1958 The Fourth Republic
1958 - present The Fifth Republic

Picture Pairs

Play Picture Pairs and see how many of the French words in this book you actually remember! The instructions given here are for two to four players, but as your French vocabulary increases, you might like to make more cards and include more players.

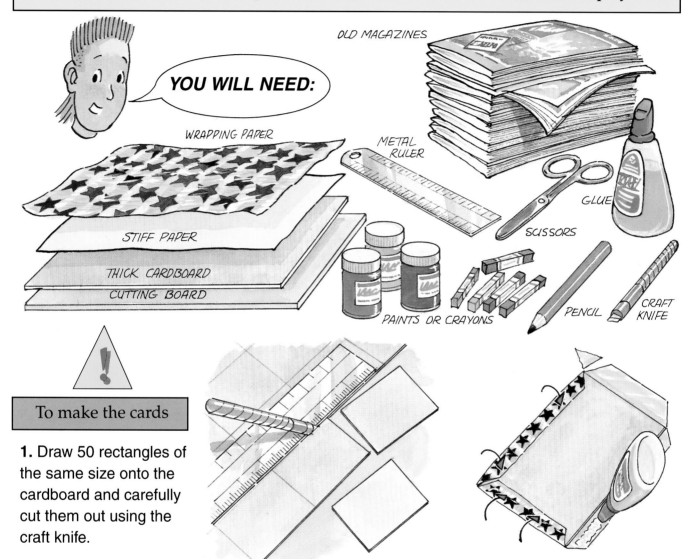

YOU WILL NEED:

OLD MAGAZINES

WRAPPING PAPER

METAL RULER

GLUE

SCISSORS

STIFF PAPER

THICK CARDBOARD

CUTTING BOARD

PAINTS OR CRAYONS

PENCIL

CRAFT KNIFE

To make the cards

1. Draw 50 rectangles of the same size onto the cardboard and carefully cut them out using the craft knife.

2. Draw another 50 rectangles onto the wrapping paper and cut them out too. These rectangles should be about $3/4$ inch (2 cm) longer and wider than the cardboard ones.

3. Cut the the corners of the paper rectangles as shown and glue them onto your cards.

4. Draw 25 rectangles, slightly smaller than your cards, onto the stiff paper and cut them out.

5. Choose 25 French words from this book and write them down with their English translations. (Keep this list beside you as you play the game.)

6. Look through the magazines and cut out any photographs that illustrate the words you have chosen. If you can't find suitable pictures, cut out some more rectangles from stiff paper and use them to paint on the pictures yourself.

les œufs

le soleil

les chaussures

le château

les vêtements

le parfum

7. Stick each photograph or picture onto the front of one of your cards. Glue the stiff paper rectangles onto the rest of the cards and write a French word from your list on each one.

To play the game
The object of Picture Pairs is to collect pairs of cards made up of words and their matching picture.

Each player starts the game with seven cards. The rest of the deck is placed face-down on the table. If you have any pairs, put them on the table in front of you.

Then ask one of the other players if he/she has a card that you need to make a pair. If that player has the card requested, he/she must hand it over and you win the pair and take another turn. If he/she does not have the card, you take a card from the deck in the middle and the turn passes to the next person.

All word cards must be translated into English. If you cannot remember the translation of the word, look it up and miss your next go.

The player who pairs all his/her cards first is the winner.

Index

Additional photographs:
Bridgeman Art Library 29; David Simpson 7(R); Eye Ubiquitous/© Jason Burke 7(T),
© F. Torrance 13(B), 28(T); Frank Spooner 4, 17(L), 18, 20(C), 21(R); J. Allen Cash 20(B), 21(B);
Renault 16(T); Rex Features 14(C),(R); Robert Harding Picture Library 12(R), 28(C); Zefa
Picture Library 6(BOTH), 7(B), 9, 12(L), 14(L), 16(B), 17(R); Visual Arts Library 26, 27.